Williamson Publishing   Charlotte, Vermor

Make Your Own
COOL CARDS
25 awesome notes & invitations!

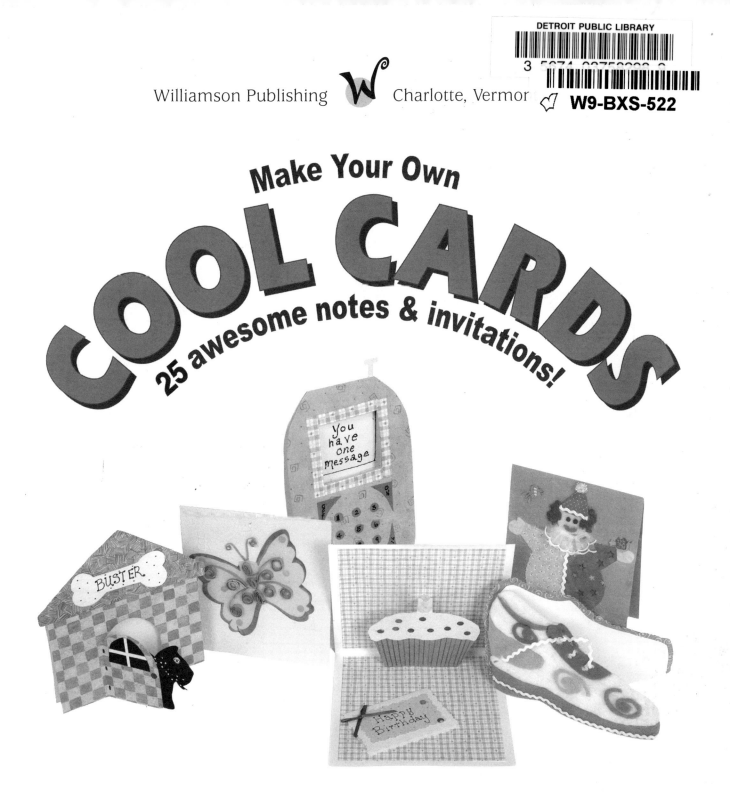

Peg Blanchette & Terri Thibault

Illustrations by Rebecca Hershey

Quick Starts for Kids!®

Library of Congress Cataloging-in-Publication Data

Blanchette, Peg, 1949–
    Make your own cool cards : 25 awesome notes & invitations! Peg Blanchette & Terri Thibault.
      p. cm. -- (Quick starts for kids)
    Includes index.
    Summary: Gives instructions for making a variety of cards and envelopes ranging from simple to more complicated shaped and three-dimensional cards.
    ISBN 1-885593-96-1 (pbk.)
    1. Greeting cards--Juvenile literature. 2. Invitation cards--Juvenile literature. [1. Greeting cards. 2. Paperwork. 3. Handicraft.] I. Thibault, Terri, 1954- II. Title. III. Series.

TT872.B555 2004
745.594'1--dc22

2003061073

Quick Starts for Kids!® series editor: **Susan Williamson**
Interior design: **Dana Pierson**
Illustrations: **Rebecca Hershey**
Cover design: **Marie Ferrante-Doyle**
Cover photography: **Karen Pike**
Printing: **Capital City Press**

Williamson Publishing Co.
P.O. Box 185
Charlotte, VT 05445
(800) 234-8791

Manufactured in the United States of America

10 9 8 7 6 5 4 3 2 1

Kids Can!®, *Little Hands*®, *Quick Starts for Kids!*®, *Kaleidoscope Kids*®, and *Tales Alive!*® are registered trademarks of Williamson Publishing.

Good Times ™, *Quick Starts Tips!* ™, *Quick Starts Jump Starts* ™, and *You Can Do It!* ™ are trademarks of Williamson Publishing.

Dedication

We dedicate this book to the "girls": our buddies Claire Aube, Linda Williamson, and Joyce Psaros. Over the years, we've encouraged each other, shared hopes and dreams, and watched our children grow. We've gone on adventures and laughed a lot. Our slumber parties are legendary! We have a bond that is as strong as family — we are like sisters, and we thank them all for their gifts of lasting friendship.

Also by Peg Blanchette & Terri Thibault

Really Cool Felt Crafts
by Peg Blanchette & Terri Thibault

Kids' Easy Knitting Projects
by Peg Blanchette

Kids' Easy Quilting Projects
by Terri Thibault

Contents

Make Them Yourself

We first started making cards when we realized how much fun it was to design them. We'd go to the card stores, look at the selections, and say to each other, "We can do that … and we can do it better!"

So we began making cards for any and all occasions. We became so well known for our creations that if we happened to be busy and bought a card for a birthday, the recipient would wonder why we hadn't hand-made one. Our cards became so popular that friends began to ask us if they could join us in our "craft room" to make some, too. We added a few more chairs, baked a few more brownies, and invited our friends over.

Our workshops have resulted in some very clever cards — along with lots of laughs and great memories shared. With scissors, glue, paper, and imagination, we've created some wild and wonderful cards (and a few wacky ones!), and we've had a whole lot of fun doing it. We haven't run out of ideas yet!

We hope that you'll use the designs in this book to make our cards into *your* cards by adding your personal and creative touches!

Peg Blanchette

Terri Thibault

A Quick Starts Guide to
Creating Cool Cards

The best thing about making your own cards is that they can be as simple or elaborate as you want them to be. The key to each unique creation lies in your imagination and what you want to express to the recipient.

A few basic supplies are really all you need — and you can substitute what you have handy for whatever we've listed below that you don't have.

Make, Gather & Buy

Assorted papers: Begin with *card stock,* which is heavier and stiffer than regular paper. Then use decorative papers in different colors, finishes, and designs.

 Buttons: Before you spend any money, check the stash of extra buttons in your home. You may find the perfect match!

Cereal-box cardboard: Use this to make templates (page 7).

Craft foam and **felt:** Sheets in assorted colors are available at craft stores.

Cutting mat: This will protect your work surface when using a rotary cutter (page 6).

Decorative items: Start with beads, feathers, felt, lace, pom-poms, ribbons, rickrack, rubber stamps, stickers, and yarn.

Fabric scraps: No need to buy these because you'll probably find lots around the house. For cards, they can be very small pieces — little snippets, really.

Glue: You'll need white craft glue, fabric glue, and hot glue (use with supervision in a hot glue gun).

Paper punch: Some of the cards use punched holes. Also, punched-out pieces of felt and construction paper make great decorations.

Pencils, pens, and **markers:** You'll need a regular lead pencil for tracing templates, as well as colored pencils, pens (try the gel-ink kind), and markers for outlining and decorating.

Rotary cutter: Use this to cut long strips of paper for quilling (page 45).

Ruler or **tape measure:** Always a handy item to have!

Scissors: In addition to craft scissors, you may want scissors with decorative edges. You can use *pinking shears,* with zigzag edges, or *edgers,* made specially for cutting decorative patterns and borders into paper. For the best cuts, all your scissors should be sharp and clean. Remember, use craft scissors on paper only; fabric scissors on fabric only.

EDGERS

Tracing paper: Use this for making templates (page 7).

Papers with Pizzazz!

One of the most exciting parts of creating a new card is picking the paper — there is so much great stuff available! It's easy to customize your card by matching the paper to the person, the occasion, and the message.

Card stock: Found in craft stores, office supply stores, art supply stores, and print shops. You can purchase blank card stock already folded and packaged with matching envelopes, or you can buy card stock (at print shops and office supply stores) and purchase or make the envelopes separately (page 8).

Decorative papers: These can be found at most craft stores. They come in a fantastic variety of colors, textures, and designs. Some of these printed papers come in a heavier weight and can be used instead of card stock.

Handmade papers: These add a touch of elegance and natural beauty. You can buy them in art and craft supply stores, or you can easily make a paper mash and add sparkles or rose petals.

Paper accents: Craft stores carry cutout shapes in small packages, but if you look before you recycle, you can probably cut and collect your own from old magazines or catalogs.

Vellum: *Vellum,* or see-through paper, can be purchased in most art and crafts supply stores. It's great for accents and special effects.

Wallpaper scraps: Perfect for card-making! Home improvement stores are a wonderful source for old wallpaper sample books.

Wrapping paper and **tissue paper:** You can create beautiful cards using the designs on wrapping paper, so open gifts slowly and save that paper!

Make Your Own Cool Cards

Keep it safe! Remember the saying, "Easy does it"? When you're using sharp scissors or a hot glue gun, play it safe — work slowly and carefully. When you're ready to use a glue gun, ask an adult to make sure you're using it correctly and to help you find a safe place to set it down while hot. Avoid touching the metal tip, which can be very hot. Make certain to unplug it when you're finished using it. A few other tips:

◎ Ask for adult help before cutting with the rotary cutter or very sharp scissors.

◎ Cover your workspace with layers of old newspaper.

◎ Store your tools and supplies where they will be safe and out of the way.

◎ Always keep small objects and sharp tools away from younger children (don't forget that they can reach what is on the edge of the table).

Getting Started

Making Templates

To make a *template* (a pattern that you can create and save in order to make your favorite cards again and again) for any of the cards in this book, follow these steps:

1. Use a pencil to trace the template patterns (pages 53 to 62) onto tracing paper. Use craft scissors to cut out the traced shapes and label them with the craft name and the part.

2. Place the tracing-paper patterns onto cereal-box cardboard. Trace around the patterns, cut them out, and label them. These cardboard pieces are now your templates.

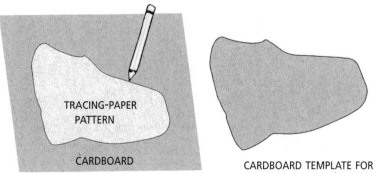

TRACING-PAPER PATTERN

CARDBOARD

CARDBOARD TEMPLATE FOR SNAZZY SNEAKERS (PAGE 62)

3. Store your cardboard templates for each project (some projects require more than one template) in a labeled envelope or zip-locking bag. That way, they'll be ready the next time you want to make the same kind of card!

Working with Measurements & Folds

Do measurements sometimes confuse you? Are you afraid you're going to fold your card the wrong way? We've made it easy for you by writing our directions the same way throughout the book, so here are some tips to remember.

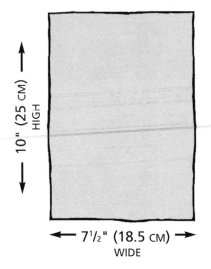

If you see directions that tell you to cut a piece of card stock 7½" x 10" (18.5 x 25 cm), you'll know to measure and cut as shown on the left.

- The **first** part of the measurement (7½"/18.5 cm) tells you how **wide** to measure and cut your card stock.

- The **second** part of the measurement (10"/25 cm) tells you how **high** to measure and cut your card stock.

Now you may be wondering, "How do I know how to fold the card?" We've described two folding methods in this book: **from side to side** and **from top to bottom**.

Let's build on the previous directions. You just cut card stock to measure 7½" x 10" (18.5 x 25 cm). The next step tells you to fold the card stock **from top to bottom**. That means you should fold it as shown here:

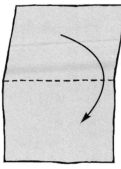

FROM TOP TO BOTTOM

But what if the directions tell you to cut card stock to measure 10" x 7½" (25 x 18.5 cm) and fold the card stock **from side to side**? That means you should cut and fold your card stock as shown here, also:

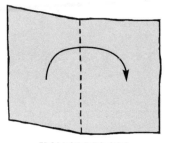

FROM SIDE TO SIDE

Making Envelopes

Homemade envelopes add to the fun — and give you an added chance to be creative. There's an easy way to make them, and as in all the projects in this book, you can dress them up any way you like. Adding stickers, stamps, and designs with gel-ink pens is always fun — as long as you leave space available for the addresses and postage.

RETURN ADDRESS

POSTAGE

LEAVE THIS SPACE FREE FOR ADDRESS

WHAT YOU NEED TO MAKE AN ENVELOPE

Large sheet of paper
Tape, for large envelope
Glue

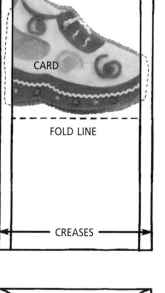

1. Lay your card in the center of the top of a large sheet of paper (computer paper will do). If your card is a large one, you can tape two sheets of paper together to make a large sheet.

2. Fold the two sides in toward the card, leaving about $1/8$" to $1/4$" (2.5 to 5 mm) on both sides of the card so it will slip in and out of the envelope easily. Crease the sheet of paper along both sides.

3. Position the card so that when you bring up the bottom part of the envelope it covers the card. Make certain you have enough paper left on top so that the top flap can fold over to cover the card and attach to the upper edge of the bottom half of the envelope.

4. Remove the card. Apply glue to the side flaps. Fold up the bottom of the envelope and press the side flaps. Let dry.

5. Insert your card. Draw a thin bead of glue along the top of the flap, fold it over the card, and press it shut along the upper edge of the envelope back. Let dry.

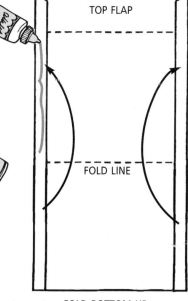

FOLD BOTTOM UP,
LEAVING A TOP FLAP

Quick Starts Tips!™

How much is enough? Remember to check your postage if you're sending a hand-made, homemade card. Even if your creation fits into a standard card envelope, the materials you used might weigh more than the usual card. The folks at the post office will be able to weigh your card and tell you which stamps you need so that the card won't be returned to you for insufficient postage.

A Quick Starts Guide to Making Cool Cards

Dazzling Dragonfly

Does your home have a button box somewhere? If not, start one because you never know when you'll be able to use them in projects such as our dragonfly card. Everyone seems to love this card — especially with the delicate vellum wings.

WHAT YOU NEED

Template supplies (pencil, tracing paper, craft scissors, cereal-box cardboard)

Card stock, cut to 9" x 7" (22.5 x 17.5 cm)

Edgers

Ruler

Decorative paper or vellum

Glue

Buttons

Black marker

Have it your way! Remember, our design is just one way of crafting this card. You can glue the buttons right to the card stock if you prefer, instead of using decorative paper. Follow your own muse! A word to the wise: Test your design to see how it looks *before* you glue anything in place.

1. Fold your card stock in half from side to side. If you'd like a decorative border, use edgers to cut around the card.

2. Cut a piece of decorative paper 3$\frac{1}{2}$" x 6" (8.5 x 15 cm). Glue it to the center of the card front.

3. Cut four wings out of vellum or contrasting decorative paper — two large top wings and two smaller bottom wings. You can use the templates on this page, or you can "wing" it!

4. Place the buttons and wings on the paper to find a dragonfly design you like. Experiment with different kinds of buttons. (Old-fashioned or pearl-like buttons look great on these cards.)

5. When you're satisfied with your design, glue the medium button in place for the "head." Glue the wings in place below the "head."

6. Where the wings meet in the center, glue the large button in place for the body. Then glue on the small buttons for the tail. Use the marker to draw antennae and a "buzzing" path below the tail.

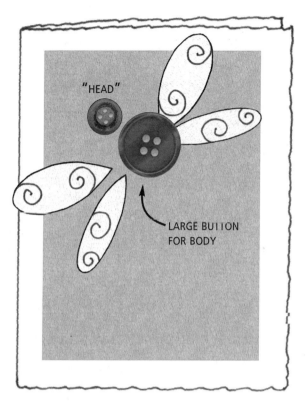

"HEAD"

LARGE BUTTON FOR BODY

Way Cool!

- If you have a lot of small buttons, make two or three dragonflies on the card front instead of one big one.
- Make it sparkle: Before attaching the wings, cover them with glue and sprinkle with fine glitter. Let dry and shake off the excess. Then glue them to the card front.

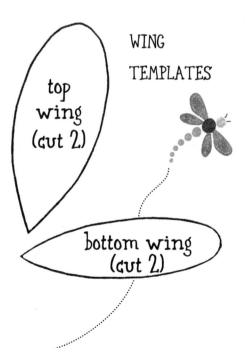

WING TEMPLATES

top wing (cut 2)

bottom wing (cut 2)

3-D Kitty

Hey, diddle, diddle,
The cat and the fiddle,
The cow jumped over
the moon ...

Maybe our kitty is following that cow as it jumps through space. Create a 3-D effect by adding easy accordion folds (below) made out of small pieces of card stock. The tail and the head can spring right off the paper!

WHAT YOU NEED

Template supplies (pencil, tracing paper, craft scissors, cereal-box cardboard)

Card stock, cut to 7" x 11" (17.5 x 27.5 cm)

Decorative paper, or rubber stamps to print a background on plain paper

Glue

Black pen

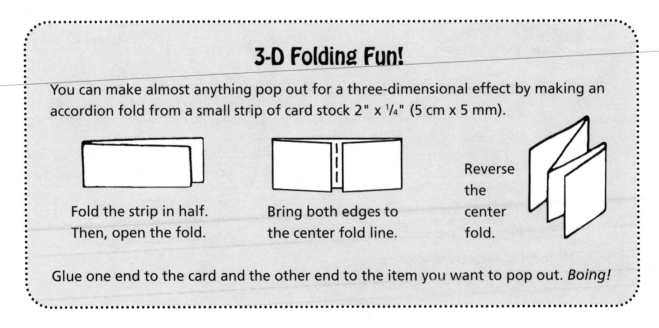

3-D Folding Fun!

You can make almost anything pop out for a three-dimensional effect by making an accordion fold from a small strip of card stock 2" x ¼" (5 cm x 5 mm).

Fold the strip in half. Then, open the fold.

Bring both edges to the center fold line.

Reverse the center fold.

Glue one end to the card and the other end to the item you want to pop out. *Boing!*

MAKING THE CARD

1. Make the three 3-D KITTY cardboard templates (page 53). See page 7 for instructions.

2. Choose a decorative paper or use a rubber stamp to put decorations onto a background. Fold the card stock in half from top to bottom.

3. Trace the BODY, HEAD, and TAIL templates onto the decorative paper. Cut out the pieces.

4. Glue the kitty's body to the card front.

5. Use the black pen to add details to the kitty's face.

6. Accordion-fold two small pieces of card stock (page 12). Glue one end of the first accordion piece to the back of the kitty's head. Glue the otherend to the body.

7. Using the second accordion piece, repeat for the tail.

Way Cool!

Make a menagerie! Use the pig template (page 53) and a squiggly, spiral tail to make a flying pig, or use the rabbit template (page 53) and a fuzzy pom-pom tail to change your jumping kitty into a scampering bunny! Draw your own heads and tails to make many different animals. Or, how about a cat jumping over the moon?

Dog in the Doghouse

Our Buster's in the doghouse, but not because he's mis-behaved! He's actually poking his head out to invite you in. If one of your friends is moving to a new home, this is the perfect card to send.

WHAT YOU NEED

Template supplies (pencil, tracing paper, craft scissors, cereal-box cardboard

2 pieces of card stock

Ruler

2 coordinating decorative papers

Glue

Black pen

Black construction paper

Scraps of white paper

Paper punch

Scraps of brown construction paper

Ribbon

GET HELP Hot glue gun/glue sticks

Coordinating Paper

We often use *coordinating*, or matching, papers to jazz up our cards. It's easy to find them because craft stores often sell them together. Coordinating papers have the same colors — they just are used in differ-ent patterns. For example, both of the papers we used for this card have a light blue background and dark blue details. The house has dark blue checks, and the roof has dark blue lines drawn in different directions. The similar colors mean that the papers go well together, but the dif-ferent details make the card more visually interesting. So, be bold, have fun, go wild as you choose your patterns and colors!

MAKING THE DOGHOUSE

1. Make the five DOG IN THE DOGHOUSE cardboard templates (page 54). See page 7 for instructions.

2. Cut a piece of card stock 5$\frac{1}{2}$" x 9" (13.5 x 22.5 cm).

3. Cut a piece of decorative paper the same size and glue it to the card stock to make the base of the house. Trim if needed. Fold the card in half from top to bottom.

4. Trace the ROOF template onto the second piece of card stock. Cut it out. Then trace the roof template onto a piece of coordinating paper. Cut out the decorative-paper roof and glue it to the card-stock roof. Trim if needed.

5. Glue the roof to the doghouse about $\frac{1}{2}$" (1 cm) below the fold line.

6. Trace the DOG BONE template onto card stock. Cut out the bone, write the recipient's dog's name on it, and glue it to the roof.

7. Lay the DOOR template in the middle of the bottom edge of the card front. Starting in the lower right corner of the door, trace up and around the door template to the notch. Cut along the traced line to the notch (make sure you cut only the card *front*).

8. Trace the WINDOW template onto black construction paper and cut out. Cut two thin strips of white paper to make divided window panes. Glue them to the window and trim as needed. Then glue the window to the top half of the door.

9. Use the paper punch to make a doorknob out of the brown construction paper. Glue the "knob" to the door. Use the black pen to draw door hinges.

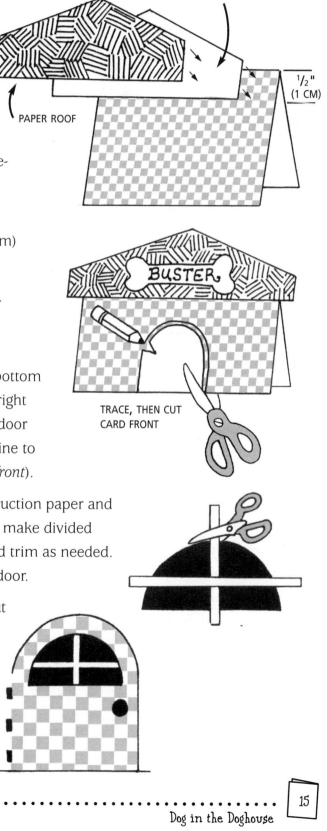

CARD-STOCK ROOF

$\frac{1}{2}$"
(1 CM)

PAPER ROOF

BUSTER

TRACE, THEN CUT
CARD FRONT

MAKING THE DOG

1. Trace the DOG template onto leftover card stock and cut it out. Then trace the dog template onto black construction paper. Glue the construction paper dog to the card-stock piece. Trim if needed.

2. Use the paper punch to make an eye from white paper, glue the eye to the dog, and decorate with a black pen.

3. Tie a thin ribbon around the dog's neck. Use a hot glue gun to glue it in place.

4. Glue the *front* of the dog to the *back* of the door so that when the door is open wide, the back of the dog is showing. (This sounds backward, but you'll see; it works!)

BACK OF THE DOG

BACK OF THE DOOR

- Why limit yourself to making a doghouse? Change the sign, remove the dog, and turn your doghouse into a pizzeria, with an arm extending out the door, holding a big slice of pizza.
- Make a clothing shop, with T-shirts on hangers or rows of shoe boxes. Cut a piece of card stock the same size as the card front (5½" x 4½"/13.5 x 11 cm). Cut a scene out of an old catalog or magazine. Glue the scene to card stock (or draw one); then glue the scene to the inside of the card front so that when you open the door the scene will show.
- Instead of making a black window, cut a window opening in the door and paste a picture of you and a friend peeking through it.

Pop-Up Cupcake

We wanted to include a pop-up card that would not only be easy to make and fun to look at, but would also put a big smile on someone's face. We think this card will do all of that — and more!

WHAT YOU NEED

Card stock, cut to 6¹/₂" x 13"
  (16 x 32.5 cm)
2 coordinating decorative papers
Craft scissors
Ruler
Glue
Template supplies (pencil, tracing paper,
  cereal-box cardboard)

Card stock for pop-up, cupcake bottom,
  icing, and mini-card
Colored pencils
Paper punch
Scraps of decorative or construction paper
Small piece of ribbon

MAKING THE CARD

1. Fold the card stock in half from top to bottom.

2. Cut out a piece of decorative paper 6" x 6" (15 x 15 cm). Glue it to the center of the card front. Cut two pieces the same size out of the other decorative paper and glue them to the top and bottom of the inside.

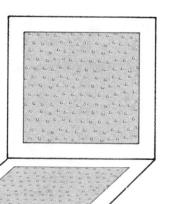

INSIDE OF THE CARD

MAKING THE CUPCAKE

1. Make the five POP-UP CUPCAKE cardboard templates (page 55). See page 7 for instructions.

2. Trace the CUPCAKE POP-UP template onto card stock. Cut it out and fold back the support tabs on the dotted lines as shown here.

3. Trace the CUPCAKE BOTTOM template onto a piece of card stock. (We used brown, but you can choose your own color.) Cut out the cupcake bottom. Use a colored pencil to draw vertical lines to resemble a paper cupcake liner.

4. Trace the ICING template onto card stock. Cut it out. Paper punch some confetti from scraps of decorative paper or construction paper. Glue them to the icing.

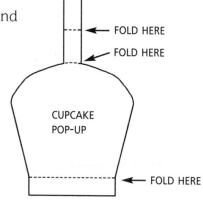

← FOLD HERE

← FOLD HERE

CUPCAKE POP-UP

← FOLD HERE

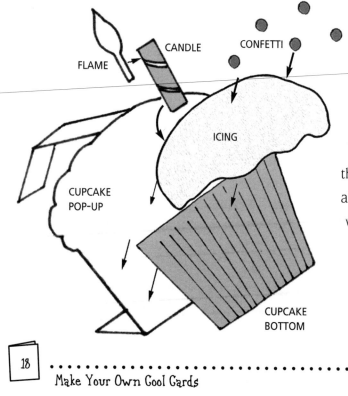

5. Trace the CANDLE and FLAME templates onto decorative papers. Cut them out. Glue the flame piece to the back of the candle. Then glue the candle between the brown card-stock cupcake bottom and the icing (you can glue it to the *front* of the cupcake bottom or the *back* of the icing). Make sure the candle stands no more than ³/₄" (2 cm) above the icing; otherwise it will stick out when the card is folded.

6. Glue the cupcake bottom to the pop-up cupcake. Glue on the icing.

7. Glue the top half of the support tab to the center of the upper half of the card interior.

8. With the card open at a 90° angle as shown below, position the bottom support tab so that the top and bottom of the cupcake are the same distance from the inside of the card. Glue in place.

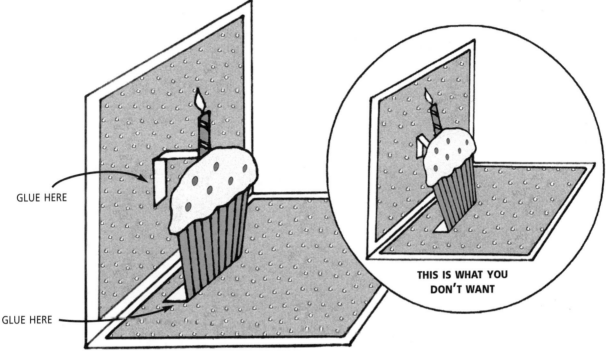

GLUE HERE

GLUE HERE

THIS IS WHAT YOU WANT

THIS IS WHAT YOU DON'T WANT

MAKING THE MINI-GREETING CARD

1. Cut a piece of card stock $3^1/_2$" x 5" (8.5 x 12.5 cm). Cut it out and fold it in half from top to bottom.

2. Cut a piece of decorative paper to cover the top of the mini-card.

3. Write your greeting on the top or on the inside.

4. To add pizzazz, glue a bow on one corner of the insert (or a sticker, appliqué, or ribbon flower).

5. Glue the mini-card to the bottom half of the inside of the card.

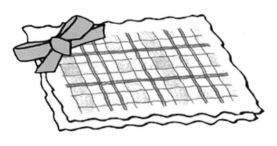

Improvise!

We used edgers to cut our decorative paper for the front of the card and the mini-card inside. Then we used craft scissors to cut the paper for the inside. You can use the same approach we did, or you can experiment with different combinations of cuts.

Fuzzy Mouse

Dryer lint is dull, gray, and dusty; it's also soft, easy to work with, and always in abundance (in most houses, anyway). When we thought of making a cute little country mouse, we didn't immediately think of dryer lint. But actually, the color and texture are perfect.

WHAT YOU NEED

Template supplies (pencil, tracing paper, craft scissors, cereal-box cardboard)

Card stock, cut to 10" x 7" (25 x 17.5 cm)

Decorative paper

Glue

Dryer lint

Toothpicks

GET HELP Hairspray (use with adult help)

Scraps of different-colored paper

Black pen

Tiny pink pom-pom or pink construction paper

Scrap of black felt or black construction paper

Ribbon

Scrap of white paper, optional

Improvise!

Don't worry if you don't have all the little bits for decoration. If you don't have a tiny pink pom-pom, use a paper punch and a scrap of pink construction paper to make a small pink dot. If you don't have black felt, use a black marker to "dot" the eye.

mouse template

MAKING THE CARD

1. Make the cardboard MOUSE template (page 20). See page 7 for instructions.

2. Fold the card stock in half from side to side. Trace the folded card onto decorative paper. Cut out the paper piece and glue it to the card front. Trim if needed.

3. Using a pencil, trace the mouse template onto the card front.

4. Fill the inside of the mouse outline with glue.

5. Gently place small amounts of lint on top of the glue. Be careful not to press down, as that will push the glue outside the traced outline.

6. Cover the entire glued area with lint, a little at a time, making sure the lint comes in direct contact with the glue. (Use a toothpick to push escaping lint back inside the lines.)

7. Let the card dry completely (overnight is best).

🐭 Go 3-D! Accordion-fold (page 12) strips of paper. Glue the strips to the backs of the balloons and the card front to make the balloons look like they're moving.

8. When the glue is dry, ask an adult to help you spray the mouse with a little hairspray.

9. Cut balloons from different papers (we used three, but you can cut as many as you like). Glue them to the card.

10. Using the black pen, draw lines connecting the balloons to the mouse.

11. Glue the pom-pom or a paper nose to the mouse. Glue on a small piece of black felt or black construction paper for the eye.

12. Tie the ribbon in a bow and glue it to the tail.

13. Cut a tiny piece of white paper and glue it below the mouse's nose for teeth. (This isn't absolutely necessary, but it makes a very nice detail.)

Ladybug Notes

Ladybugs are everywhere. They're on fabric, rubber boots, garden accessories, and paper goods. They're climbing on walls and chairs — on just about everything. But our ladybug does something most cannot: It becomes something else (but you'll have to read on to find out what).

WHAT YOU NEED

Template supplies (pencil, tracing paper, craft scissors, cereal-box cardboard)

Tape

Card stock, cut to 8$\frac{1}{2}$" x 11" (21 x 27.5 cm)

2 coordinating decorative red papers

Glue

Black construction paper

Paper punch

Scrap of white paper

Silver gel-ink pen, optional

Black pen

Ruler

MAKING THE CARD

1. Make the three LADYBUG NOTES cardboard templates (page 56). See page 7 for instructions.

2. Tape the bug BODY and WINGS templates together along their long, straight edges. Trace this large template onto card stock and cut out.

3. Fold the card stock from top to bottom where the two templates were joined.

WINGS TEMPLATE

TAPE HERE

BODY TEMPLATE

Make Your Own Cool Cards

4. Carefully remove the tape to separate the bug body and wings templates. Trace the bug body template onto one piece of red paper and cut out. Glue the red paper piece to the *inside* of the card. Trim if needed.

5. Trace the wings template onto a coordinating piece of red paper and cut out. Glue the paper piece to the card front to decorate the wings. Trim if needed.

6. Trace the HEAD template onto the black construction paper and cut it out. Glue the paper head to the back of the card $^{1}/_{2}$" (1 cm) below the fold.

7. Cut black circles from the construction paper and glue them on the wings in any pattern you like.

8. Use a paper punch to make two white dots for "eyes" (you can also use a silver gel-ink pen). Use a black pen and ruler to draw lines on the inside for your message.

DECORATIVE PAPER ON CARD FRONT (WINGS)

FOLDED CARD STOCK

GLUE HEAD TO BACK OF CARD SO THE CARD'S FOLD LINE HITS THE DOTTED LINE ON THE HEAD AS SHOWN

DECORATIVE PAPER ON INSIDE OF CARD (BUG BODY)

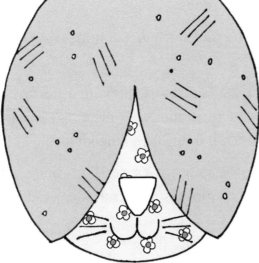

From bug to bunny! To transform your ladybug into a loveable little bunny, just pick different colored papers, add a nose cut out of construction paper, and draw a mouth and whiskers! For totally cool whiskers, try gluing on pieces of yarn or thick thread.

Pool Party Invitation

Summertime is a fun time to create wonderful memories of barbeques and pool parties. The splashing, the laughing, the lounging — it doesn't get any better! If you don't have a pool, have a "cool off" party, using a water hose or sprinkler for fun times together.

WHAT YOU NEED

Template supplies (pencil, tracing paper, craft scissors, cereal-box cardboard)

Card stock, cut to 10" x 7" (25 x 17.5 cm)

Decorative paper

Craft foam

Ribbon

Ruler

GET HELP ▷ Hot glue gun/glue sticks

Sequin trim

Scrap of colored paper

Pen or marker

MAKING THE CARD

1. Make the four POOL PARTY INVITATION cardboard templates (page 25). See page 7 for instructions.

2. Fold the card stock in half from side to side.

3. Trace the folded card onto the decorative paper. Cut out the paper piece and glue it to the card front. Trim if needed.

4. Trace the BIKINI TOP, BIKINI BOTTOM, and SANDALS templates onto craft foam and cut out the pieces.

5. Cut three pieces of ribbon 2" (5 cm) for the bikini-top neck and side straps. Use the hot glue gun to glue the ribbon pieces to the *back* of the bikini top.

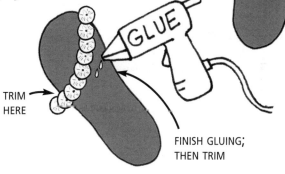

GLUE HERE

GLUE HERE

BACK OF BIKINI TOP

6. Cut two pieces of ribbon 2" (5 cm). Make two bows and glue them to the *front* of the bikini bottom — one on each side, as shown on the finished card.

TRIM HERE

7. Cut two short pieces of sequin trim. Using a hot glue gun, glue them to the tops of the sandals. Trim to fit. Cut another piece of sequin trim. Use a hot glue gun to glue it along the neckline of the bikini top.

8. Cut a small square from a scrap of colored paper and write the words "Pool Party" on it.

GLUE

9. Arrange your "Pool Party" square, the foam suit, and the sandal pieces on the card front. Use a hot glue gun to glue them in place. (See page 38 for what to write inside the card.)

TRIM HERE

FINISH GLUING; THEN TRIM

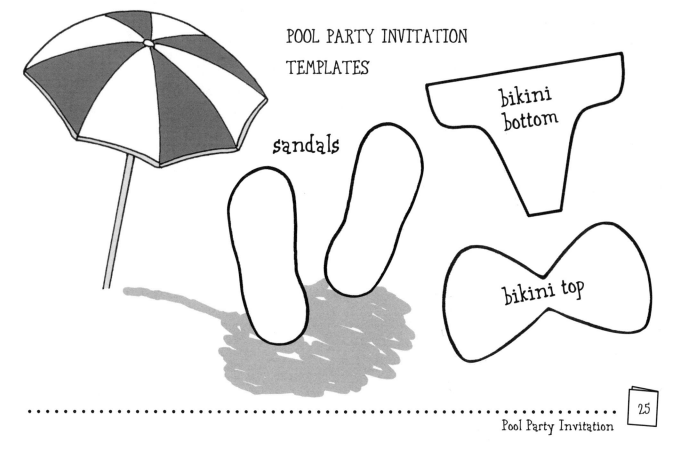

POOL PARTY INVITATION TEMPLATES

sandals

bikini bottom

bikini top

Foamie Flower Basket

We love working with craft foam. It's fantastic; it's easy to cut; it comes in bright colors; and it bends, twists, and stays in place when it's glued. You may not need any templates to make the flowers because you'll have fun coming up with your own shapes and designs, but we included a couple below, just in case!

WHAT YOU NEED

Template supplies (pencil, tracing paper, craft scissors, cereal-box cardboard)

Card stock, cut to 11" x 7" (27.5 x 17.5 cm)

Ruler

Decorative paper

Edgers

Glue

Craft foam in assorted colors

HELP ▶ Hot glue gun/glue sticks

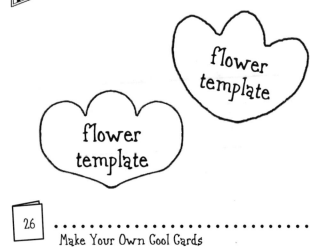

flower template

flower template

MAKING THE CARD

1. Make the three FOAMIE FLOWER BASKET cardboard templates (page 57). See page 7 for instructions.

2. Fold the card stock in half from side to side.

3. Use edgers to cut a piece of decorative paper 5" x 6¹/₂" (12.5 x 16 cm). Glue the paper to the center of the card front.

4. Trace the BASKET template onto a sheet of craft foam. (We used dark brown, but you can choose what you'd like.) Cut out the foam basket.

Make Your Own Cool Cards

5. Fold the foam basket in half from side to side. Cut slits for weaving as shown. Be sure not to cut through the edges.

6. Trace the WEAVING STRIP template three times onto a piece of craft foam in a contrasting color. (We used light brown, but you can select your own color.) Cut out the strips and weave them through the basket slits.

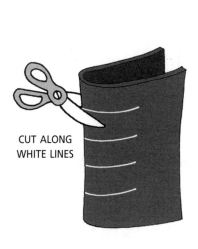

CUT ALONG
WHITE LINES

7. Trim the strips to the edges of the basket and use a hot glue gun to glue the ends in place.

8. Trace the HANDLE template onto a piece of contrasting craft foam and cut it out.

9. Using a hot glue gun, glue the basket to the card front along the sides and bottom of the basket. Leave the top edge unglued.

GLUE
HERE

TRIM HERE;
THEN GLUE

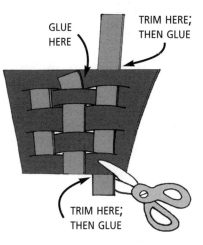

TRIM HERE;
THEN GLUE

LEAVE OPEN

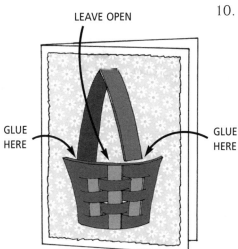

GLUE
HERE

GLUE
HERE

10. Fold the basket handle in half and use a hot glue gun to glue the two ends to the card underneath the top edge of the basket.

11. Cut out flowers, leaves, and stems from different-colored pieces of craft foam.

12. Arrange them in your basket. Overlap them for a 3-D effect. Use a hot glue gun to glue in place.

Fall into autumn! You can easily change this basket of summer posies into a bushel of scrumptious autumn apples. Simply leave off the top handle and use red craft foam to make apples instead of flowers. Yum!

Fabric Clown

Who can resist a clown? They make people smile, cheer them up, and lift their spirits. Your clown card will accomplish all of that and more — because it's homemade and because it's from you.

WHAT YOU NEED

Template supplies (pencil, tracing paper, craft scissors, cereal-box cardboard)
Card stock, cut to 12" x 5" (30 x 12.5 cm)
Scraps of different fabrics
Fabric scissors
Scrap of tan felt
Scraps of black and red felt
Yarn for hair
Fabric glue
Lace scrap
Rickrack
Pom-poms

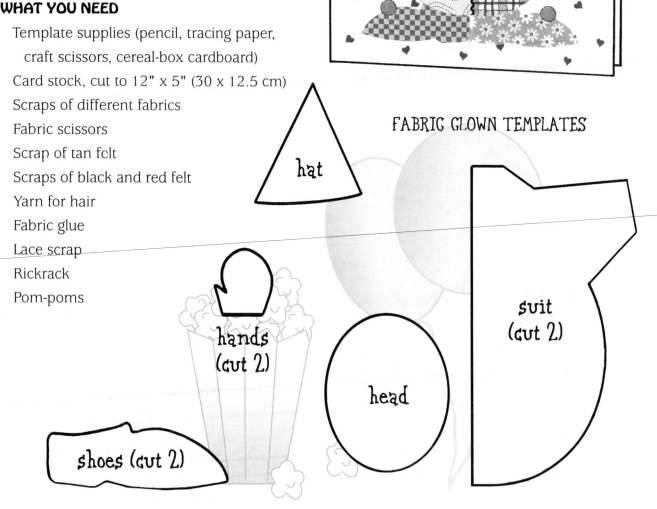

FABRIC CLOWN TEMPLATES

hat

hands (cut 2)

head

suit (cut 2)

shoes (cut 2)

MAKING THE CARD

1. Make the five FABRIC CLOWN cardboard templates (page 28). See page 7 for instructions.

2. Fold the card stock from side to side.

3. Lay the SUIT, SHOES, and HAT templates on your choice of fabrics (the brighter, the better). Trace and cut out.

4. Lay the HEAD and HANDS templates on tan felt. Trace and cut out.

5. Cut two dots out of black felt for eyes. Cut a smile out of red felt for the mouth.

6. Cut bits of yarn for the hair.

7. Place your fabric and felt pieces on the card front to make an arrangement you like. Then, glue all of your pieces in the following order:

    ◎ fabric shoes
    ◎ fabric suit
    ◎ felt head
    ◎ felt hands
    ◎ rickrack trim down front of suit
    ◎ lace collar
    ◎ felt eyes and mouth
    ◎ yarn hair
    ◎ fabric hat
    ◎ rickrack trim on hat
    ◎ pom-poms for shoes and hat

Quick Starts Tips!™

Fabric: right or wrong? Every piece of fabric has two sides: a *right* side and a *wrong* side. The right side looks like the finished material, such as the bright, printed side of a cotton print. The wrong side is the faded side of the fabric or the back, like the inside-out side of a shirt or dress. When working with the fabric on this project, the following tips will help you cut your pieces just the way you want them.

1) Before you trace your templates, lay the brighter, *right* side of the fabric against the work surface so you are tracing the template onto the faded, *wrong* side.

2) Some of the templates require that you cut two pieces. To make sure that both pieces show the right side of the fabric after you cut them, trace one, then flip it to trace the other, as shown.

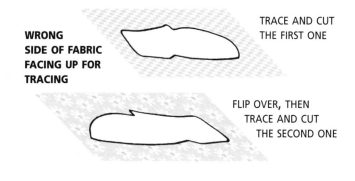

WRONG SIDE OF FABRIC FACING UP FOR TRACING

TRACE AND CUT THE FIRST ONE

FLIP OVER, THEN TRACE AND CUT THE SECOND ONE

Way Cool!

❀ If you'd like to add details to your card, you can cut them out of fabric scraps that may have little clown-related "doo-dads" on them. It adds some extra clown fun. Stickers are also an option since there are many wonderfully detailed stickers available now.

Special Delivery Pop-Out

We've shown you our pop-up design (page 17). Now for our pop-OUT design. This card is fun to make because of all the possibilities it presents! You can adapt it to any occasion: Add a diploma for a graduation, a gift box or flower bouquet for a birthday or Mother's Day, a baseball glove or book for Father's Day or Dad's birthday. If you think you can't draw, you can always use pictures of items cut out of old magazines, catalogs, or calendars.

WHAT YOU NEED

Card stock, cut to 8¹/₂" x 6¹/₂" (21 x 16 cm)

Ruler

Decorative papers in assorted colors

Craft scissors

Edgers, optional

Glue

Scraps of card stock

Pen or marker

Template supplies (pencil, tracing paper, cereal-box cardboard)

Colored pencils

Scraps of green construction paper

Paper punch

Improvise!

We decorated our "hand-out" with a shirtsleeve and cuff made of paper, but you can color it in or decorate it with tiny beads to make a bracelet. What other hand-out designs can you think of?

Make Your Own Cool Cards

MAKING THE CARD

1. Fold the card stock in half from side to side.

2. Measure a piece of decorative paper $3\frac{3}{4}$" x 6" (9.5 x 15 cm). Use edgers or craft scissors to cut it out.

3. Glue the decorative paper to the center of the card front. Glue a smaller piece of card stock on top of the decorative paper.

4. Write the words "Special Delivery" or your own personal greeting on the top layer.

MAKING THE POP-OUT

1. Make the five SPECIAL DELIVERY cardboard templates (page 57). See page 7 for instructions.

2. Trace the pop-out support template onto card stock. Cut it out. Fold it in half and then in half again to make four sections. Then fold to make a box as shown.

3. Open the card at a 90° angle. Glue section A to the upright side of the card, halfway down the fold. Make sure the edge of section A sits along the fold of the card.

4. Glue section D to the bottom of the card. Make certain that the edge sits along the fold of the card.

5. Press in place until the glue sticks. Then leave the card at a 90° angle and let dry.

MAKING THE "HAND-OUT"

1. Trace the ARM/HAND template onto card stock. Cut it out. Trace the SHIRTSLEEVE, CUFF, and VASE templates onto decorative paper. Cut them out.

2. Glue the shirtsleeve and cuff, as shown (or simply color them if you prefer).

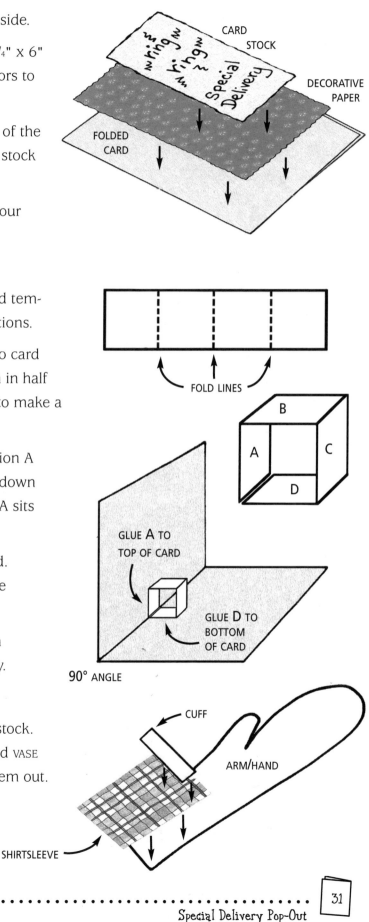

Special Delivery Pop-Out

3. To make stems, snip thin, short strips from scraps of green construction paper. (Keep them short so they don't show above the card when it's closed.) Glue the stems to the back of the vase.

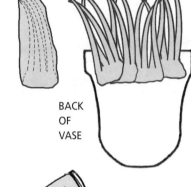

BACK
OF
VASE

4. Cut flower shapes out of decorative paper. Use a paper punch to make centers for the flowers. Glue the centers in place. Glue the flowers to the stems.

5. Holding the arm/hand piece, slip the vase in back of the thumb. Then, add a few drops of glue to the *right* side of the vase and wrap the tip of the hand around the front of the vase to glue the fingertips to the front.

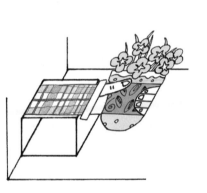

ADD GLUE AND THEN
FOLD HAND OVER

6. Draw finger and fingernail details. Glue the finished arm/hand piece to the top of the pop-out support.

Good luck at your new school!

Congratulations!

Way Cool!

✿ "Hand" someone a book: Cut a small piece of card stock (sized to fit inside the hand) and decorate it to look like a book cover; or glue a few pieces of paper in between a small, folded piece of card stock to make a tiny book!

✿ Roll up a piece of paper, tie it with a ribbon, and "hand" your friend a diploma.

✿ Make a set of keys for someone who's just passed her driving test.

Cell Phone Invitation

You won't need a lot of technology to make this cell phone card, and it will be a big hit with everyone! It can be used the way we made this one — as a party invitation — or you can turn it into a thank-you note, a get-well card, a message of congratulations, a birthday greeting, or an announcement. The list is endless. If there's a reason to send a card, this one is lots of fun!

you
have
one
message

OFF

ON

SPKR

Pull
DOWN

Simon Peters
is having a
Birthday Party
Saturday, June 20
32 Gilson Lane
2:00 – 5:00
RSVP 555-6061

you
have
one
message

Pull
Down

WHAT YOU NEED

Template supplies (pencil, tracing paper, craft scissors, cereal-box cardboard)

Card stock, 8$\frac{1}{2}$" x 11" (21 x 27.5 cm)

2 coordinating decorative papers

Glue

Paper punch

Scrap of construction paper

Ruler

Pen or thin marker

MAKING THE CARD

1. Make the four CELL PHONE INVITATION cardboard templates (page 58). See page 7 for instructions.

2. Trace the CELL PHONE template onto card stock. Cut it out and fold it in half.

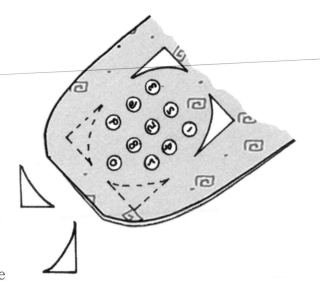

3. Trace the folded cell phone card onto a piece of decorative paper. Cut out the paper piece and glue it to the card front.

4. Open the card and cut a window in the card front, as shown on the template (page 58).

CUT WINDOW THROUGH PAPER AND CARD STOCK ON FRONT ONLY

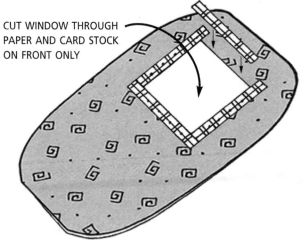

5. Cut four thin strips of coordinating decorative paper to frame the window; glue them in place.

6. Use a paper punch to make "phone buttons" out of the construction paper. Glue them in place and write numbers on them.

7. Cut four small triangles out of construction paper. Glue them, as shown, and write "on," "off," "spkr," and "mail" (or other words you would like on them).

8. Trace the SIDE GUIDE template two times onto card stock. Cut them out. Trace the STOP PLATE template onto card stock. Cut it out.

9. On the lower half of the inside of the card, glue one of the side guides along the left side of the card, as shown (page 35). Make sure you run the glue along the edge of the card only, so that the message board can easily slide between them. Glue the other side guide along the right side, as shown. If the edges don't match exactly, trim as needed.

10. Position the bottom stop plate ¼" (5 mm) above the bottom edge of the card, as shown. Glue the side edges only, leaving the top and bottom of the stop plate open so the message board tab can slide through it. Let the side guides and bottom stop plate dry.

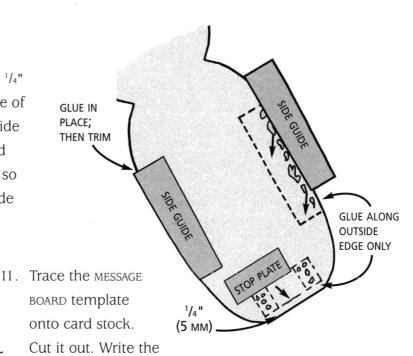

GLUE IN PLACE; THEN TRIM

SIDE GUIDE

SIDE GUIDE

GLUE ALONG OUTSIDE EDGE ONLY

STOP PLATE

¼" (5 MM)

11. Trace the MESSAGE BOARD template onto card stock. Cut it out. Write the words "Pull Down" at the bottom of the message board tab. Open the card and slide the message board tab through the stop plate and the two side guides.

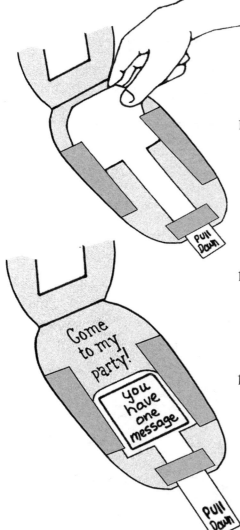

Come to my party!

you have one message

Pull Down

Pull Down

12. Close the card. Push the message board tab up toward the fold until it won't move. (The top of the message board should now be against the inside fold line.) When the message board is in place, use a pen or thin marker to trace the window opening onto the message board; write part of your message here.

13. Open the card and write the rest of your message on the top of the phone. Pull the message board all the way down and write an additional, surprise message in the space shown.

14. Cut a small antenna piece out of card stock. Glue it to the back of the folded card.

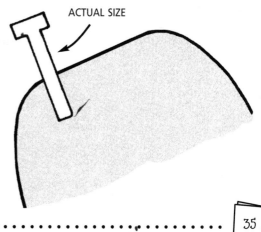

ACTUAL SIZE

Sleepover Invitation

Lots of kids love slumber parties — preparing the snacks, getting the games ready, picking out the right music and videos, giggling and having fun. If you've never hosted a sleepover party before, now's the time! This invitation is easy to make, and it says, "Let's have a great time!"

WHAT YOU NEED

Template supplies (pencil, tracing paper, craft scissors, cereal-box cardboard)

Card stock, 8¹/₂" x 11" (21 x 27.5 cm)

Decorative paper or felt

Glue

Edgers, optional

Coordinating paper

Paper punch

Ribbon or yarn

Ruler

Scraps of light colored paper

Colored pencils

MAKING THE SLEEPING BAG

1. Make the two SLEEPOVER INVITATION cardboard templates (page 59). See page 7 for instructions.

2. Trace the SLEEPING BAG template onto the card stock. Cut it out. Then trace the sleeping bag template onto decorative paper or felt. Cut it out and glue it to the card stock. If you like, use edgers to trim the sides and neckline of the card.

DECORATIVE PAPER OR FELT

CARD STOCK

3. Cut a piece of coordinating paper 3" x 2" (7.5 x 5 cm) to make a pillow for the inside of the sleeping bag. Trim the pillow with edgers, if you like, and glue to the inside of the bag.

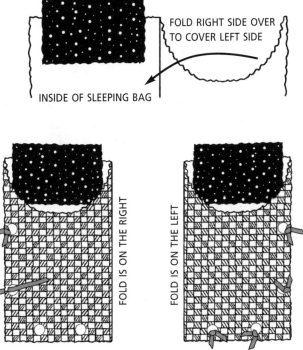

FOLD RIGHT SIDE OVER TO COVER LEFT SIDE

INSIDE OF SLEEPING BAG

4. Fold the card in half from side to side to form the bag, with the decorative paper showing on the outside. Use the paper punch to make two holes on the open side and two holes along the bottom.

5. Cut four pieces of ribbon or yarn, each approximately 3" (7.5 cm). Thread them through the holes and tie to close the bag.

FOLD IS ON THE RIGHT

FOLD IS ON THE LEFT

THIS WAY ALSO WORKS

Quick Starts Tips!™

Either way is OK! You may be wondering why we pictured the sleeping bag with the fold on *either* the right *or* the left. It all depends on how you traced the template and on which side of the card stock you glued your decorative paper. It doesn't really matter which way you fold your bag — as long as the decorative paper shows on the outside.

Way Cool!

✸ Cut out a picture of your face or a favorite character and draw a fun body. Make photocopies, cut them out, and slip them inside the sleeping bags.

It's All in the Details!

When you write a party invitation, don't forget to include all the information your guests might need to know.

Who: Of course, you know who is sending the invitation — you are! But the recipient won't know unless you write your name on the invitation.

What: Is this a birthday party? Graduation party? End-of-season soccer team party?

When: This includes the day, date, and time.

Where: Write down the location of the party. If it isn't a familiar place to all of your friends, you may want to have an adult help you write out directions on a separate piece of paper. You can include a copy of the directions with your invitation.

What to bring: This may be especially helpful if it's a sleepover or a swim party.

A number to call: Your friend or an adult may have questions about the party.

An "R.S.V.P.": If you would like to know how many guests will be coming, you can ask that they let you know if they can attend. The letters R.S.V.P. are from the French phrase *respondez s'il vouz plez,* which means "please respond."

MAKING THE PAPER DOLL

1. Trace the PAPER DOLL template onto a piece of paper. Cut it out. Lay the piece of paper over the pattern on page 59 to trace the clothing and body details onto your paper doll. Use colored pencils to fill in. Or, you can draw your own details instead of tracing (page 37).

2. On the reverse side of your paper doll, write your invitation. (Drawing lines with a ruler first before you write may make it a little easier and neater.) Don't forget the details above!

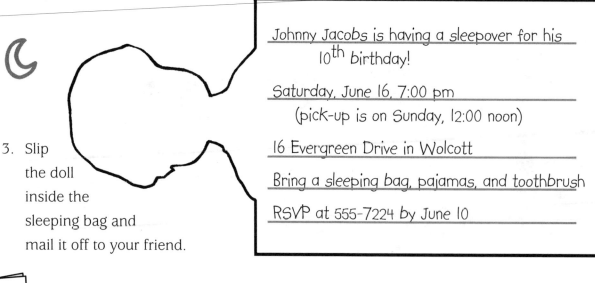

Johnny Jacobs is having a sleepover for his 10th birthday!

Saturday, June 16, 7:00 pm
(pick-up is on Sunday, 12:00 noon)

16 Evergreen Drive in Wolcott

Bring a sleeping bag, pajamas, and toothbrush

RSVP at 555-7224 by June 10

3. Slip the doll inside the sleeping bag and mail it off to your friend.

Jazzy Purses

Send a pal her own purse, and you'll be amazed at her reaction. Last year we made 25 of these as party invitations (each one was different), and we couldn't believe how much people loved them. Our friend Betsy decided to frame some of the purses she made and give them as gifts, which we thought was a great idea!

PURSE A

PURSE B

WHAT YOU NEED

Template supplies (pencil, tracing paper, craft scissors, cereal-box cardboard)

Tape

2 pieces of card stock: 5$\frac{1}{2}$" x 10" (13.5 x 25 cm) for Purse A, 5$\frac{1}{2}$" x 12" (13.5 x 30 cm) for Purse B

Decorative papers

Glue

Ribbon

Ribbon rose, button, sticker, or beads

MAKING PURSE A

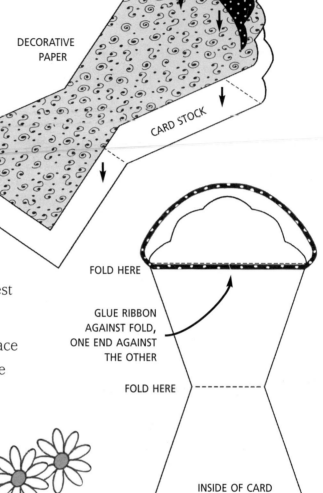

FRONT FLAP

DECORATIVE PAPER

CARD STOCK

1. Make the two Jazzy Purse A cardboard templates (page 60). See page 7 for instructions.

2. Trace the PURSE A template onto the piece of card stock. Cut it out.

3. Trace the PURSE A template onto decorative paper. Cut out the paper piece. Glue it to your card. Trim if needed.

4. Trace the FRONT FLAP template onto a coordinating paper. Cut it out and glue it to the front flap.

5. Fold the card twice — once at the narrowest point and once at the widest point.

6. Cut a piece of ribbon 12" (30 cm) long. Place the two ends of the ribbon inside along the upper fold line. Glue it in place.

7. Add decorative trim to the outside flap.

FOLD HERE

GLUE RIBBON AGAINST FOLD, ONE END AGAINST THE OTHER

FOLD HERE

INSIDE OF CARD

MAKING PURSE B

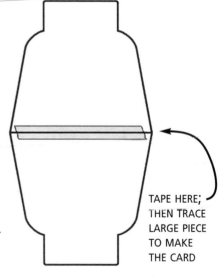

TAPE HERE; THEN TRACE LARGE PIECE TO MAKE THE CARD

1. Make both of the cardboard templates (page 41). See page 7 for instructions.

2. Tape the two PURSE B templates together along the widest edges as shown to make a large purse template.

3. Trace the large purse template onto a piece of card stock to make your card. Cut it out.

4. Trace the large purse template onto decorative paper. Cut out the paper piece. Glue it to the card front. Trim if needed.

Make Your Own Cool Cards

5. Open the card and lay it on your workspace so the card-stock side (the inside) is facing up. Trace the HANDLE template on both the top and bottom of the card, as shown.

6. Cut out the **bottom** handle on *all four sides.* Cut the **top** handle along *both sides and the top line only.* Leave the bottom line uncut.

7. Fold the card in half. To make the latch, fold the flap on the back part of the handle through the opening on the front part of the handle. Trim to fit if it's too large. Decorate the front latch.

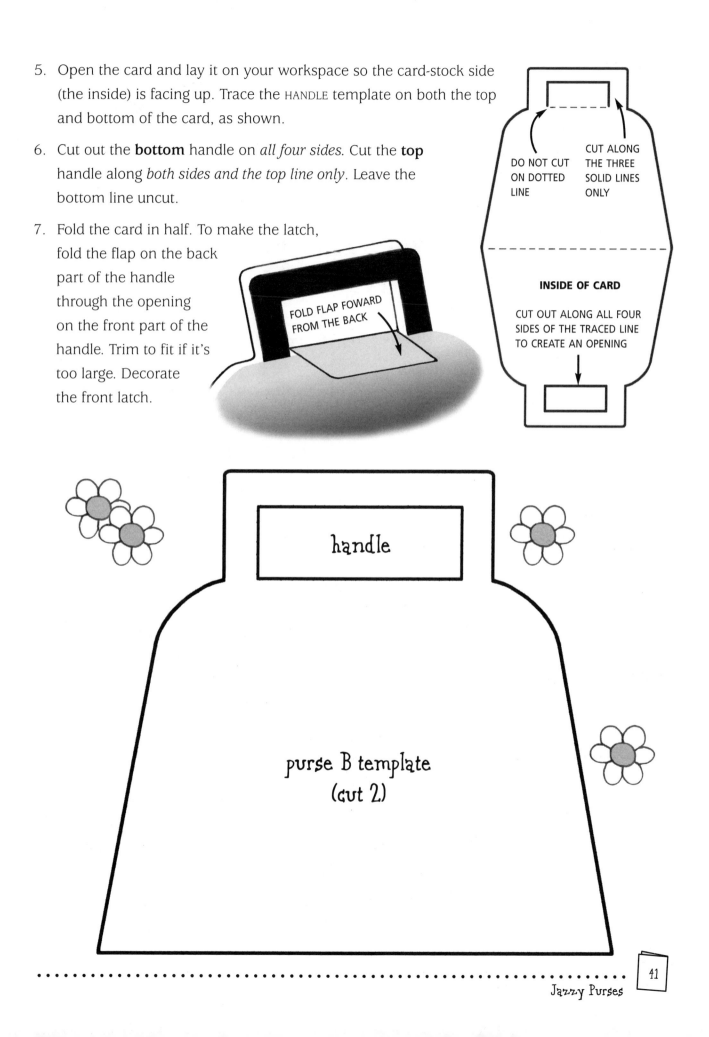

DO NOT CUT ON DOTTED LINE

CUT ALONG THE THREE SOLID LINES ONLY

INSIDE OF CARD

CUT OUT ALONG ALL FOUR SIDES OF THE TRACED LINE TO CREATE AN OPENING

FOLD FLAP FOWARD FROM THE BACK

handle

purse B template
(cut 2)

Button Blossoms

By saving scraps of fabric and paper, along with old buttons, you can create one-of-a-kind greeting cards that anyone would be happy to receive. The cheery button blossoms on this card will make smiles happen. These are more than homemade cards — they convey thoughts from your heart that will be cherished!

WHAT YOU NEED

Card stock, cut to 11" x 7¹/₂"
   (27.5 x 18.5 cm)
Scissors: craft scissors, pinking
   shears, and edgers
Ruler
Green ribbon
Scraps of fabric or decorative
   paper
2 coordinating decorative
   green papers
Glue
Buttons

Improvise!

When we made our card, we used one fabric for each flower, making six petals from the same fabric. Try something different: Add more petals and use contrasting fabric or decorative paper for petals on the same flower.

MAKING THE CARD

1. Fold the card stock in half from side to side.

2. Use craft scissors to cut two ribbon stems — one 3" (7.5 cm) and one 4" (10 cm).

3. Use pinking shears to cut 12 petals out of the fabric or decorative paper — six for each flower.

4. With the craft scissors, cut four leaves out of one of the green decorative papers (two leaves for each flower).

5. Position the stems, petals, and leaves on the card front. Glue in place.

6. Glue a button in the center of each flower.

7. Cut a strip of the second green paper 5$\frac{1}{2}$" x 1$\frac{1}{2}$" (13.5 x 3.5 cm). Use edgers to cut along the top edge in a wavy pattern.

8. Use craft scissors to make small snips along the top edge of the paper for the grass detail.

9. Glue the bottom edge of the grass strip (below the snips) to the card front. Create a "grassy" look by feathering the snips so they don't lay flat against the card.

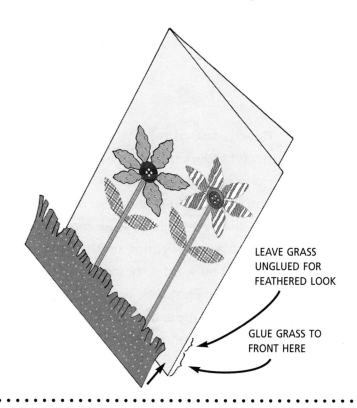

LEAVE GRASS
UNGLUED FOR
FEATHERED LOOK

GLUE GRASS TO
FRONT HERE

Improvise!

Find a bug-shaped button or cut out a picture of a bug to glue to the grassy area. Or, draw your own bug. The fun in making these cards is that there are no rules — just let your creative spirit hang loose!

Quilled Creations

This decorating method looks harder than it really is. By mixing different quilled shapes, you can create an original work of art that begs to be displayed! Our design uses two simple shapes — loose circles and loose scrolls — but you can add other shapes to give your card even more visual and textural interest.

WHAT YOU NEED

2 pieces of card stock: 5¹/₂" x 12" (13.5 x 30 cm) for butterfly card, 7¹/₂" x 5¹/₂" (18.5 x 13.5 cm) for flower card

Template supplies (pencil, tracing paper, craft scissors, cereal-box cardboard)

Vellum

Colored marker

Quilling strips (page 45)

Toothpick or quilling tool

Ruler

GET HELP Hot glue gun/glue sticks

Tweezers, optional

Paper punch

Scrap of construction paper

Glue

Decorative paper or fabric scraps

Scrap of green construction paper

Quick Starts Tips!™

Ready, set, glue! Hot glue dries fast, so you need to work quickly! That's why it's always a good idea to have your shapes made before you start to glue. Once you have them made, you'll also be able to work more quickly if you then place everything on the card, exactly where you want it, before you begin gluing pieces on. That way, you can just lift a piece, apply your glue, and quickly replace the piece exactly where you want it to go.

The Art of Quilling

Quilling, also known as paper filigree, is a very old art form, going back approximately 500 years. Quilling involves rolling very thin strips of paper and then pinching the rolled paper into assorted shapes. It got its name because people used goose *quills* (feathers) to roll the paper shapes.

There are many common quilling shapes, but we used only the loose circle and loose scroll. We like these shapes because they don't require pinching, but you can experiment with other shapes and add them to your card design.

| TIGHT CIRCLE | LOOSE CIRCLE | TEARDROP | SHAPED MARQUISE | STAR | LOOSE SCROLL | OPEN HEART SCROLL | HALF HARP |

To quill, you'll need long, thin strips of paper. Specially made quilling paper can be purchased in craft stores, but if you have a rotary cutter, cutting mat, and ruler, an adult can help you cut the thin strips from your own stash of paper. We used strips of card stock, but you can use a lighter weight paper if you like. If you're using paper you have at home, experiment with one or two strips before you begin making your quilled pieces. This way, you'll know if it will roll well and hold its shape.

Making the shapes

Begin with strips that are ³⁄₈" (7.5 mm) wide and 12" (30 cm) long. Cut as many strips as you'll need for your project. (Make a few extra in case you make a mistake with one or two.)

Start the quill by wrapping it around a very thin object. You can buy a quilling tool, but a toothpick works just as well. Finish by hand, pulling it into a tight spiral as you go.

Put a drop of glue where you want the roll to stop.

You're all done! If you want to experiment with different shapes, pinch the curled pieces between your fingers to form the shapes.

LOOSE CIRCLE

LOOSE SCROLL

MAKING THE BUTTERFLY

1. Fold the card stock in half. (We did a top-to-bottom fold for ours, but you can fold side to side if you like.)

2. Trace the BUTTERFLY template along the black line onto vellum paper; cut it out.

3. Run a thick marker all the way around the border of the vellum butterfly to make an outline. (We used a light blue vellum paper with a dark blue marker, but you can experiment with different colors.)

4. Make the following rolled pieces:

   (We used blue paper, but you can use any color you like.)

   3 loose circles
   4 loose scrolls with one end 1¹/₂" (3.5 cm) long
   4 loose scrolls with one end ¹/₂" (1 cm) long

   Place your pieces on the vellum butterfly, as shown in the pattern above. You can make it easy by placing your vellum butterfly over the pattern to make certain your pieces are in the right place.

5. First, use a hot glue gun to glue the three loose circles down the middle (a set of tweezers can be helpful here). Hold the circles in place until the glue dries.

6. Next, glue the four long scrolls in place.

7. Finally, glue the four short scrolls in place.

8. Use a paper punch to make dots from the construction paper. Glue them to the wings.

9. Glue the spine of the butterfly to the card so the wings remain loose. Make two antennae out of quilling strips. Use the hot glue gun to attach the antennae above the spine.

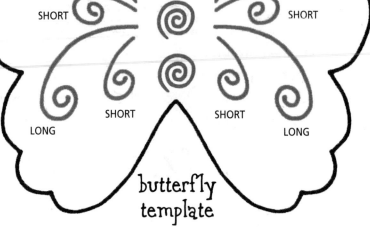

LONG LONG
SHORT SHORT
SHORT SHORT
LONG LONG

butterfly template

LONG SCROLL   SHORT SCROLL

MAKING THE POT OF POSIES

1. Make cardboard templates for the flower-pot and saucer below. See page 7 for instructions.

2. Fold the card stock in half from side to side.

3. Trace the FLOWER POT and SAUCER templates onto decorative paper or fabric scraps and cut them out.

4. Glue the flowerpot to the card front. Leave the top edge of the flower pot open, gluing the sides so the flowerpot forms a kind of pocket in the middle, where you will tuck the rolled ends. Then glue the saucer to the bottom of the flowerpot.

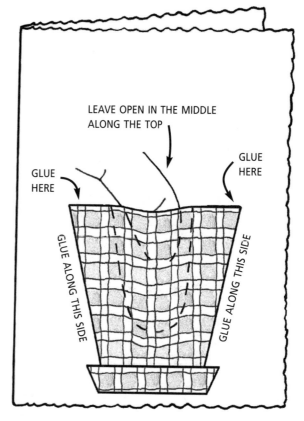

LEAVE OPEN IN THE MIDDLE ALONG THE TOP

GLUE HERE

GLUE HERE

GLUE ALONG THIS SIDE

GLUE ALONG THIS SIDE

LOOSE SCROLLS

LOOSE SCROLLS

LOOSE SCROLL

LOOSE SCROLL

flowerpot template

saucer template

5. Make the following rolled pieces out of quilling strips that match your flowerpot paper: (We used yellow for the loose circles and purple for the loose scrolls, but you can use any color you like.)

   4 loose circles
   6 loose scrolls of various lengths

6. Cut six small leaves out of the green paper. Then place the leaves and rolled pieces on your card front, as shown in the pattern or in some other pattern you want to try.

7. Glue the leaves in place.

8. Tuck the ends of the six loose scrolls inside the opening of the flowerpot. Glue each one in place.

9. Finally, glue the four loose circles in place.

Stars in Cars

We love taking pictures, so we decided to incorporate that hobby into our card-making. We started with this little "car" and three of our favorite faces, but our next photo card will be a stretch limo with lots of windows!

WHAT YOU NEED

Template supplies (pencil, tracing paper, craft scissors, cereal-box cardboard)

Card stock, cut to 7½" x 10" (18.5 x 25 cm)

Decorative paper or construction paper

Glue

Photos of your friends or family

Scraps of black and gray construction paper

Stickers and colored pencils

MAKING THE CARD

1. Make the four STARS IN CARS cardboard templates (page 61). See page 7 for instructions.

2. Fold the card stock in half from top to bottom.

3. Place the CAR template on the card stock with the top of the car on the fold line. Trace the template onto the card stock and cut through both layers of card stock to make the "car." Be careful not to cut through the fold.

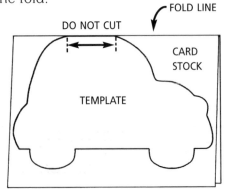

4. Trace the CAR template onto decorative or construction paper. Cut out the paper car. Cut out two "windows" on the decorative paper similar to the windows shown on page 61. Glue the paper car to the card front *below* the window openings only.

5. Cut the faces from photos you have chosen. Lift up the paper on the top half of the card and position the faces in the "windows."

SLIDE THE PHOTOS BEHIND THE PAPER AND SET INTO PLACE

FRONT OF CARD

INSIDE OF CARD

GLUE DECORATIVE PAPER TO THE CARD FRONT IN THIS AREA, BELOW THE WINDOWS

6. Glue the photos to the card stock so they show through the "windows." in the paper. Let dry. Then glue the top half of the paper to the card front.

7. Trace the WHEEL templates onto black construction paper. Cut them out. Cut two smaller circles out of gray construction paper. Glue them to the black wheels. Glue the black wheels to the card.

8. Trace the FENDER and HEADLIGHT templates (page 61) onto decorative or construction paper. Cut them out and glue them to the card front.

9. Now beautify your "car" with stickers or drawings!

Snazzy Sneakers

Here's your chance to design your own line of sneakers! There are no limits — so have fun! If you don't have any felt, use white and colored papers. No rickrack? Use yarn, colored string, or a real shoelace!

WHAT YOU NEED

Template supplies (pencil, tracing paper, craft scissors, cereal-box cardboard)

Card stock, cut to 13¹/₂" x 5¹/₂" (33.5 x 13.5 cm)

White felt square

Scraps of different colored felt

Fabric glue

Pinking shears, optional

Rickrack

Ruler

Paper punch

Decorative paper, optional

MAKING THE CARD

1. Make the five SNAZZY SNEAKERS templates (page 62) as shown. See page 7 for instructions.

2. Fold the card stock in half from side to side. Place the large sneaker template on the folded card stock against the fold as shown. Trace the template onto the card stock and cut through both layers of card stock — except on the fold line — to make your card base.

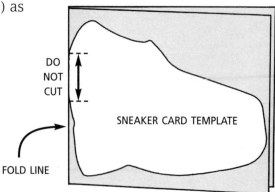

DO NOT CUT

SNEAKER CARD TEMPLATE

FOLD LINE

3. Trace the SNEAKER BASE template onto the felt square. Cut the shape from the felt and glue the piece to the card front.

4. Place the SNEAKER SOLE, BACK PIECE, and SHOELACE GUIDE templates onto felt scraps. (We used a different color for each one, but you can design your own color scheme.) Cut them out. Glue the sneaker sole and back piece to the card front (do not glue the shoelace guide yet). If you want your sneaker to look as if it has tread, cut along the bottom of the card front with pinking shears after the sneaker sole has been glued on.

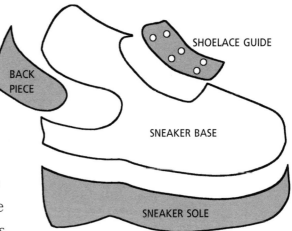

5. Cut two pieces of rickrack 1" (2.5 cm) long. On the shoelace piece, use a paper punch to make six holes through which to lace your rickrack shoelaces. Thread the two short pieces through the bottom two pairs of holes. Glue the ends to the *back* of the shoelace guide and trim if needed.

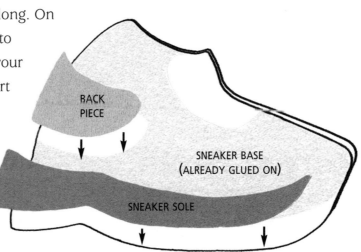

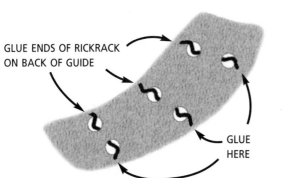

BACK OF SHOELACE GUIDE

GLUE ENDS OF RICKRACK ON BACK OF GUIDE

GLUE HERE

FRONT OF SHOELACE GUIDE

TIE RICKRACK AT TOP OR LEAVE LOOSE

Then cut one piece of rickrack 4¹/₂" (11 cm) long. Tie it through the holes at the top of the shoelace guide. Leave it loose or make a bow. Now glue the shoelace guide to the card front.

6. To make your sneaker snazzy, cut out three felt spirals (or more if you wish) and glue them to the card front.

   Cut a thin curved strip about 2" (5 cm) long out of scrap felt and glue it as shown to make the opening.

TO MAKE A SPIRAL, START WITH A CIRCLE; THEN CUT AS SHOWN.

TRIM AS SHOWN IF YOU WANT A THINNER SPIRAL PATH

THIN CURVED STRIP

THIN CURVED STRIP TO MAKE OPENING

7. Cut a piece of rickrack 7" (17.5 cm) long. Glue it across the sneaker sole and trim if needed.

8. Make circles and stars from assorted felt scraps and glue them below the rickrack strip on the sneaker sole.

RICKRACK

RIGHT SIDE OF PAPER

WRONG SIDE OF PAPER

TRACED SNEAKER TEMPLATE (TURNED OVER)

CUT 1/4" (5 MM) *OUTSIDE* THE TRACED TEMPLATE

9. If you would like to add a decorative paper background to the card, turn the sneaker template over and trace it onto the *wrong* side (page 29) of a piece of decorative paper. Cut out the piece 1/4" (5 mm) outside the traced line. Glue the paper to the back of the card so that the *right* side faces front.

OPEN CARD WITH DECORATIVE PAPER SHOWING TO THE FRONT

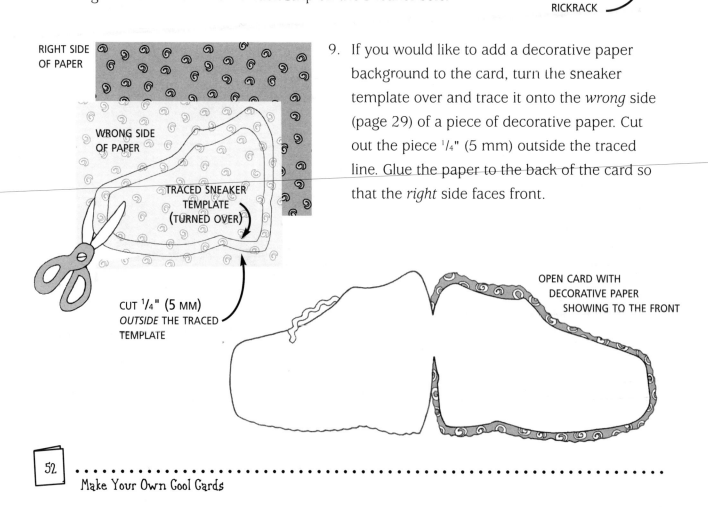

Templates

kitty body

kitty head

3-D Kitty

kitty tail

pig

rabbit

Dog in the Doghouse

window

door

dog

dog bone

roof

Make Your Own Cool Cards

bottom

candle & flame

cupcake pop-up

icing

Pop-Up Cupcake

Ladybug Notes

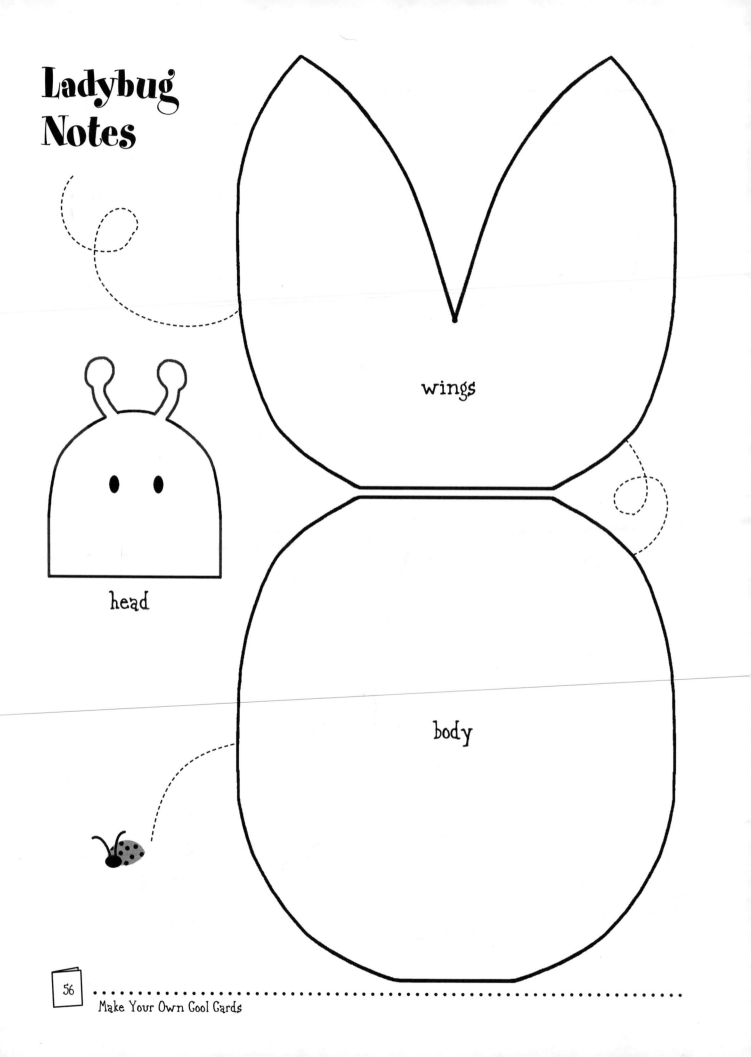

head

wings

body

Make Your Own Cool Cards

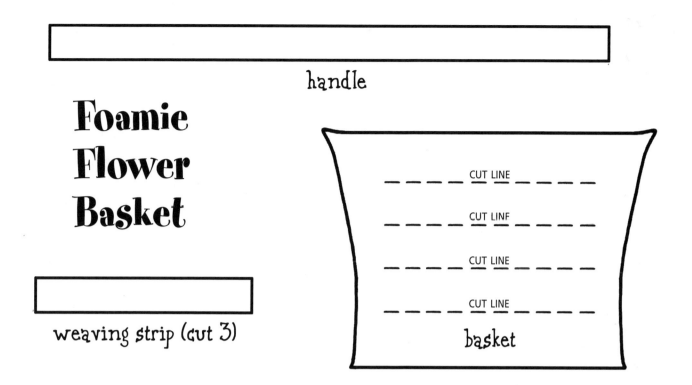

Foamie Flower Basket

handle

weaving strip (cut 3)

CUT LINE

CUT LINF

CUT LINE

CUT LINE

basket

Special Delivery Pop-Out

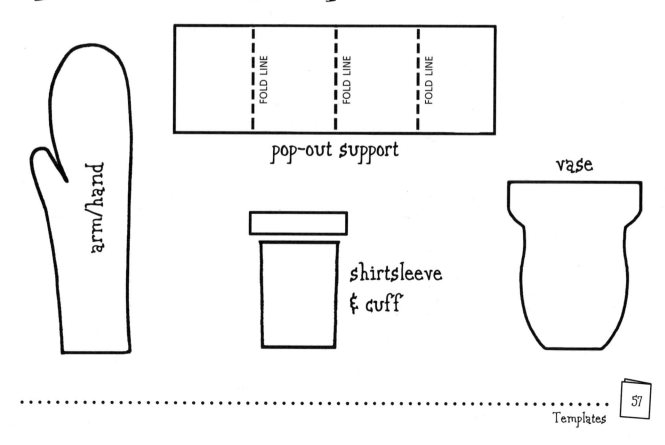

FOLD LINE FOLD LINE FOLD LINE

pop-out support

arm/hand

shirtsleeve & cuff

vase

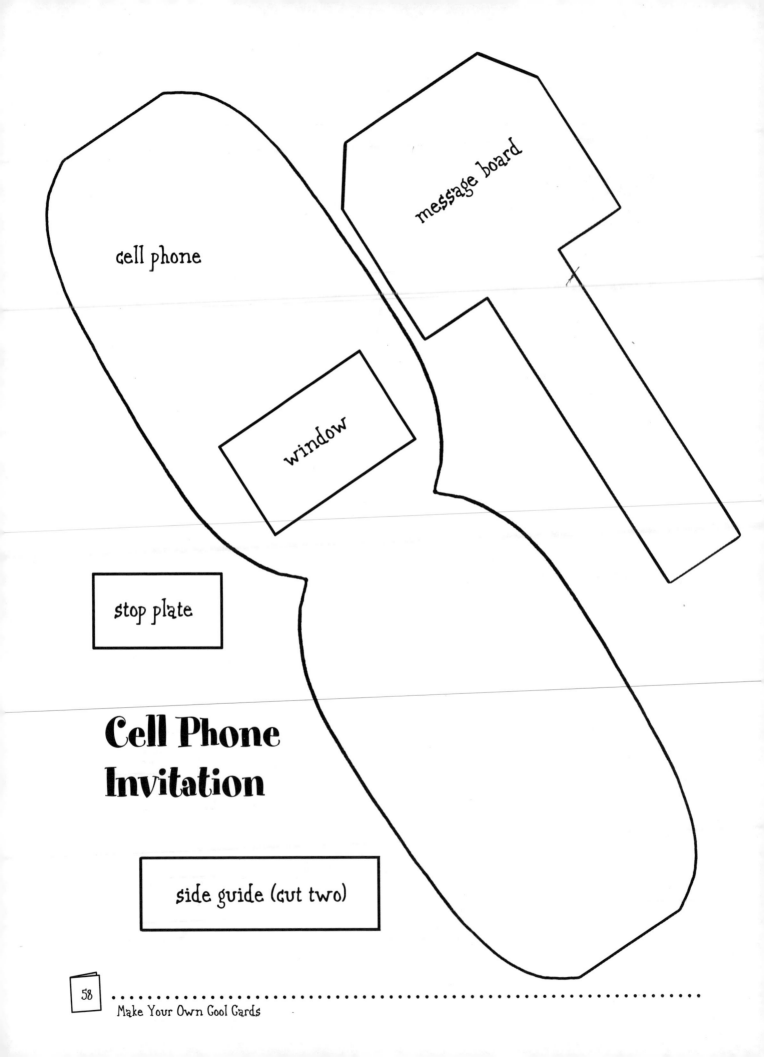

cell phone

message board

window

stop plate

Cell Phone
Invitation

side guide (cut two)

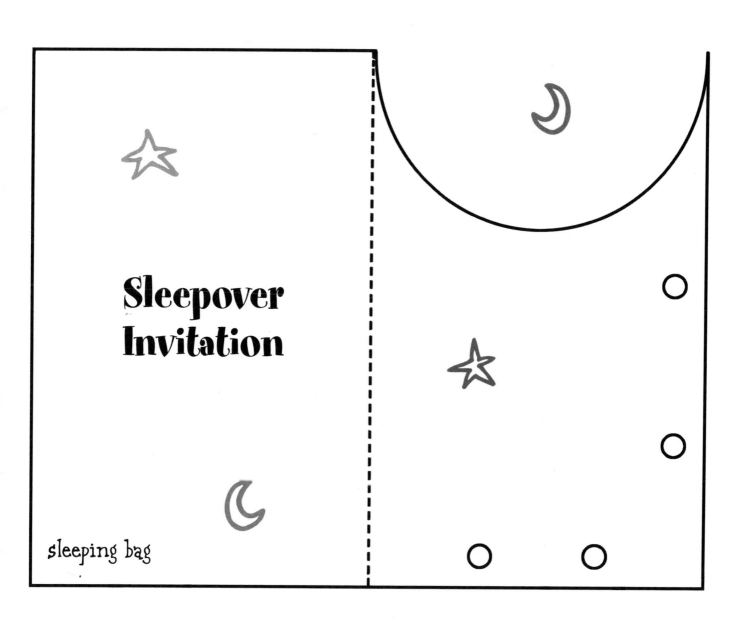

Sleepover
Invitation

sleeping bag

paper doll

Jazzy
Purse A

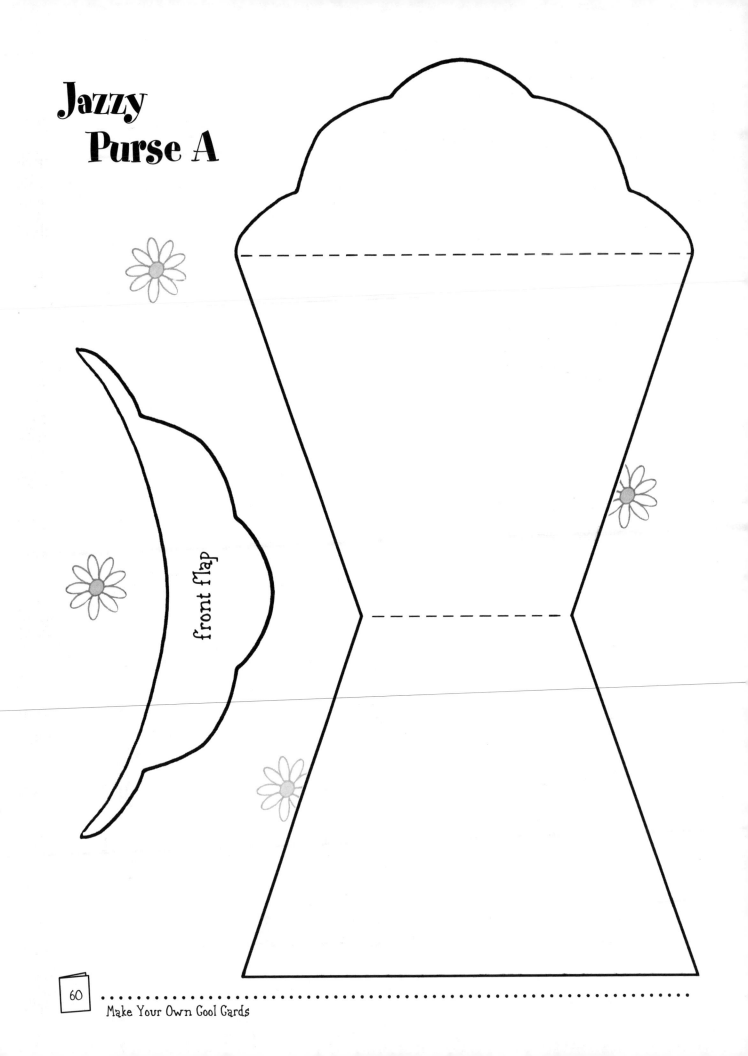

front flap

Make Your Own Cool Cards

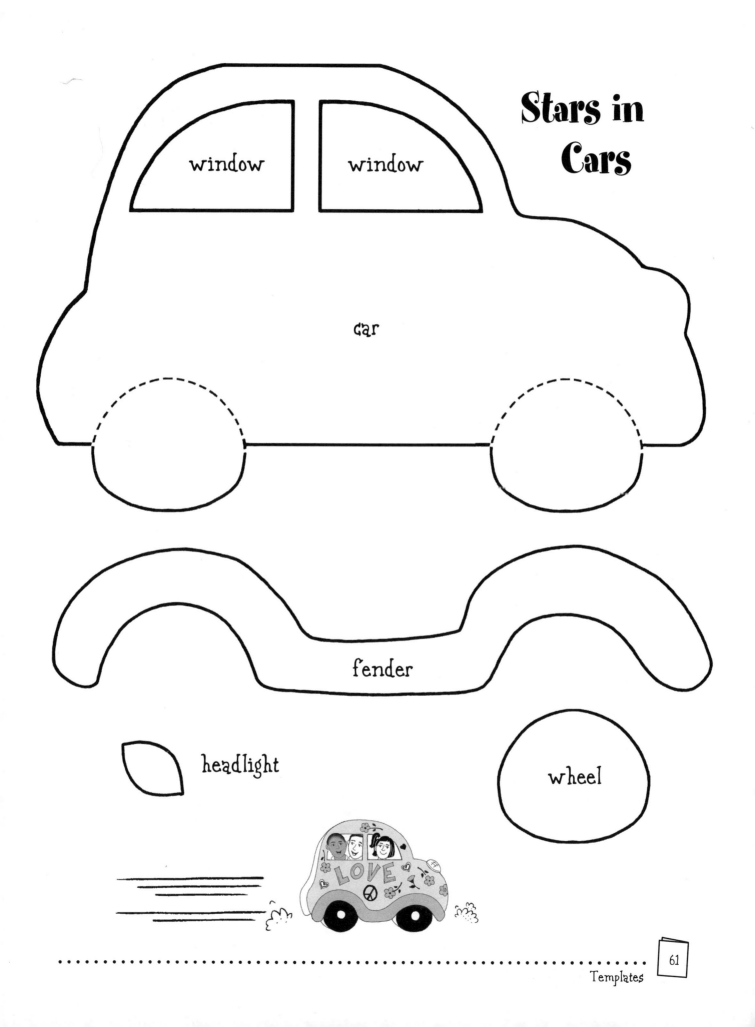

Stars in Cars

window window

car

fender

headlight

wheel

Snazzy Sneakers

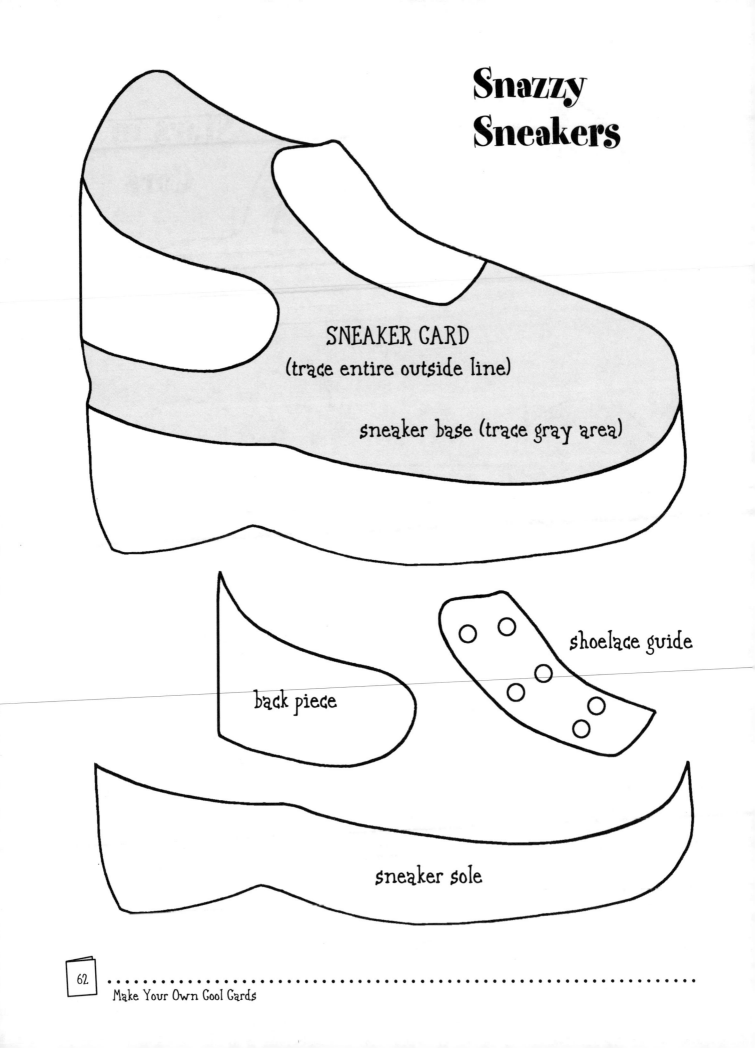

SNEAKER CARD
(trace entire outside line)

sneaker base (trace gray area)

back piece

shoelace guide

sneaker sole

Make Your Own Cool Cards

Index

More Good Books from Williamson Publishing

Quick Starts for Kids!®
Books for ages 8 to adult are each 64 pages, fully illustrated, trade paper, 8½" x 11", $8.95 US/$12.95 CAN.

REALLY COOL FELT CRAFTS
by Peg Blanchette & Terri Thibault

KIDS' EASY KNITTING PROJECTS
by Peg Blanchette

KIDS' EASY QUILTING PROJECTS
by Terri Thibault

EASY-TO-MAKE CANDLES
by Laura Check

MAKE YOUR OWN CHRISTMAS ORNAMENTS
by Ginger Johnson

ALMOST-INSTANT SCRAPBOOKS
by Laura Check

MAKE YOUR OWN HAIRWEAR
Beaded Barrettes, Clips, Dangles & Headbands
by Diane Baker

MAKE YOUR OWN FUN PICTURE FRAMES!
by Matt Phillips

Parents' Choice Approved
BAKE THE BEST-EVER COOKIES!
by Sarah A. Williamson

Oppenheim Toy Portfolio Gold Award
DRAW YOUR OWN CARTOONS!
by Don Mayne

DRAWING HORSES (that look *real!*)
by Don Mayne

American Bookseller Pick of the Lists
MAKE YOUR OWN TEDDY BEARS & BEAR CLOTHES
by Sue Mahren

KIDS' EASY BIKE CARE
Tune-Ups, Tools & Quick Fixes
by Steve Cole

40 KNOTS TO KNOW
Hitches, Loops, Bends & Bindings
by Emily Stetson

Dr. Toy 10 Best Socially Responsible Products
Dr. Toy 100 Best Children's Products
MAKE YOUR OWN BIRDHOUSES & FEEDERS
by Robyn Haus

GARDEN FUN!
Indoors & Out; In Pots & Small Spots
by Vicky Congdon

CREATE A YEAR-ROUND WILDLIFE HABITAT
For Urban & Suburban Small Spaces
by Robyn Haus

BE A CLOWN!
Techniques from a Real Clown
by Ron Burgess

YO-YO!
Tips & Tricks from a Pro
by Ron Burgess

Visit Our Website!
www.williamsonbooks.com

And More ...

Williamson's Kids Can!®
Books for ages 7 to 14 are each 128 to 176 pages, fully illustrated, trade paper, 11" x 8½", $12.95 US/$19.95 CAN.

Parents' Choice Recommended
KIDS' ART WORKS!
Creating with Color, Design, Texture & More
by Sandi Henry

Benjamin Franklin Education/Teaching Gold Award
Parent's Guide to Children's Media Award
HAND-PRINT ANIMAL ART
by Carolyn Carreiro

Parents' Choice Gold Award
American Bookseller Pick of the Lists
THE KIDS' MULTICULTURAL ART BOOK
Art & Craft Experiences from Around the World
by Alexandra M. Terzian